T0209910

"Through Our Good and Bad"

Prayer is Power

Kisha "Kee" Rhames

Scripture quotations taken from the Holy Bible, New Living Translation, Copyright © 1996, 2004. Used by permission of Tyndale House Publishers, Inc., Wheaton, Illinois 60189. All rights reserved.

WestBow Press books may be ordered through booksellers or by contacting:

WestBow Press
A Division of Thomas Nelson & Zondervan
1663 Liberty Drive
Bloomington, IN 47403
www.westbowpress.com
1 (866) 928-1240

ISBN: 978-1-4908-5981-1 (sc)
ISBN: 978-1-4908-5982-8 (e)

Library of Congress Control Number: 2014920431

Printed in the United States of America.

WestBow Press rev. date: 12/22/2014

WESTBOW
PRESS
A DIVISION OF THOMAS NELSON
& ZONDERVAN

"Through Our Good and Bad"

Prayer is Power

Acknowledgement of God

God is the creator, the beginning and end, Alpha & Omega, and the finisher. God is above all things and nothing is impossible for Him. The 66 Books illustrate all you need for your life journey. God has many attributes. God is Trinity of the Omni's: 1. Omnipotent- All Power, 2. Omniscience- All Knowing All the Time, and 3. Omnipresent- Everywhere.

About Me

I would first like to thank God, who is ahead of my life, for being saved and filled with the Holy Spirit. Thank God for giving me the strength, ability, vision, power, and mind set to write encouraging motivational words to share with the world. My name is Kisha Rhames and I am originally from Brooklyn, New York. You can call me "Kee". Growing up in Brooklyn, Bedford Stuyvesant on Van Buren St, I have enjoyed every moment being mommy's only girl with two brothers. I was raised to be the empowering woman I am today by my mother and grandmother. I have a father, step-father, two brothers, two step-brothers, and five step-sisters. I have an immediate family who consisting of a son, daughter, and significant other. I like to pray, read the bible, write, communicate with people, assist with cooking, have fun, encourage others, exercise, spend time with family, and play board games. I have a heart's desire to help anyone in need as the spirit leads me. I am currently working towards receiving my Associate of Science Degree in Medical Assistance. I will find a way to bring back together those that are odds with each other within my family, friends, and acquaintances, after praying and being still for God. Life is too short to be angry about anything when we have God who is greater than any situation.

Introduction:

I was compelled to write this book because we all need to be uplifted while on our daily journey in this life with God's guidance. The encouraging motivational words are not only for everyone else, but for me as well so that I may continue to be the mother, future wife, sister, role model, spiritual believer, and friend I need to be according to HIS WILL. The words from God are God's word provided to me for the people and myself. God speaks to me through life experiences and through communicating with others across the world on their daily life journey. It is easy to encourage everyone else until oneself has to "walk the walk" after talking the talk. I have been writing encouraging words three times a week since I was 23, and never thought "my words" could be for a book. I have moved to Kuwait in February 2010 and I began to engage in writing daily. I had started sending text messages out to seven people a day after communicating with them on their situations and circumstances. The next month, thirty people were receiving the daily encouraging word. News about what I was doing was spreading through the grapevine and soon, others were asking to receive the text messages. People would come up to me and say, "Kee, I saw several texts from you on encouraging words on your journey, may I receive it too"? I started thinking to myself this is serious and people are actually taking the time to read my texts. All of these encouraging words were truly from God because people would say that seemed as if they told me their life story or situation. We know God is real when we can encourage, or motivate someone when they going through a rough time and they did not tell us anything about what is going on in their life. I can testify to going through some things and to seeing the reality of the Bible while walking on this daily journey and interacting with people. Nothing is new under the sun.

The journey of writing this book was not hard, or easy; it was a tunnel I had to crawl through and I am still in the tunnel. LOL. It took being still, observant, patient, loving, humble, interactive, walking by faith, and believing that if this is for me, God will give me all I need to accomplish His mission for the people and myself. We all go through the good and the bad, but are we willing to hold on knowing we have God who is the Almighty and has all power. Sometimes we make bad decisions, It does not mean we are bad people - it means we should learn from those bad decisions and face whatever circumstance lead to those decisions. I know that without God, I could not write these words 365 days a year alone. The journey has just begun and I know God has much more in store. I fall short of the glory of God at times as well, and I have truly learned through my experiences; the God I know who brought me this far, has never left me, even when I thought there was no way. God has agape love for us even when we don't deserve it. Thank God for everything. People ask me how do I listen to people all day, encouraging them mentally, emotionally, physically and spiritually? My answer is the Love of God. Also, when someone comes to me, I ask "Are you here to vent or receive my opinion?" Depending on their answer, I will say, "Lord, have your way." God already knows who He is sending to me that day. However, I must also be the natural judge on some situations and I will know that by being lead by the Holy Spirit God has equipped in me. What God has created and designed in me is my gift from Him and NO MAN can take it. I must keep my anointing covered daily. What I do for Jesus will last forever.

No matter what happened yesterday, know and believe we can make a difference today. Smile in spite of the situation. Enter the book with expectancy for your life journey.

Table of Contents

Daily Faith Wheel

"Sinners Soul"

Sinners have a soul. A sinner is someone that is not saved by grace of the blood of Jesus. A born again Christian sin but they are not a sinner. We don't judge and talks about a sinner but continue to pray for them and encourage them to become a born again child of God. We suppose to spread the good gossip. No one is perfect but we strive to be Christ like.

John 3:16

For this is how God loved the world: He gave his one and only Son, so that everyone who believes in him will not perish but have eternal life.

"Let it Go"

Let your day be rejoicing and let God handle all your problems because we can't do it alone. "Let it go". You can try but nothing will get accomplished the same problem will persist. Let it go and let GODS plan work in your favor. "Respect what you accept".

Proverbs 3:5-6

Trust in the Lord with all your heart; do not depend on your own understanding. Seek his will in all you do, and he will show you which path to take.

Self Check

Sometimes we ask ourselves, why people treat me this way? Why no one get along with me? Why I am always having a bad day? First we need to reassure ourselves by doing a self evaluation with God's help by praying and seeking him for understanding in life.

2 Corinthians 13:5

Examine yourselves to see if your faith is genuine. Test yourselves. Surely you know that Jesus Christ is among you; if not, you have failed the test of genuine faith.

Reflection of You

One thing to keep in mind is what you do is your business. What you do reflects you. What you don't tell-the world won't know. God knows all and is all. God will bring the best out of you. When we look at our reflection, we should see God in us. His light should be shining on us, and then reflecting off us.

2 Corinthians 3:16-18

But whenever someone turns to the Lord, the veil is taken away. For the Lord is the Spirit, and wherever the Spirit of the Lord is, there is freedom. So all of us who have had that veil removed can see and reflect the glory of the Lord. And the Lord—who is the Spirit—makes us more and more like him as we are changed into his glorious image.

Blessed and Highly Favored

No it's not just a cliché! What does this truly mean to be "blessed and highly favored"? It simply means to be

Obedient to Him- Have Faith in Him- Know Him- Wait on Him

God has favored you. It's up to you to make Him your favorite and receive what all He has in store for you. You are favored. Don't worry about what everybody else maybe saying around you. God has favored you.

Psalm 90:17

And may the Lord our God show us his approval and make our efforts successful. Yes, make our efforts successful!

Got Faith?

Our faith, at times can become unsteady because of the different trials and tribulations we face, but do we continue to stand firm on our faith? God test our faith at times to allow us to see do we really trust and depending on Him like we say we are and as the WORD says we ought. Pray through all the trials and tribulations to strengthen your faith and trust in God. Now watch how God begins to move in your life.

James 1:3

For you know that when your faith is tested, your endurance has a chance to grow.

Focus on You

Do you find yourself at times worrying about what everybody else is doing or not doing verses focusing on getting yourself together? We have to stay in our lane without focusing on the next person, and better ourselves with Gods assistance. If you are finding fault in everyone else, you are more likely to be doing the same thing but can't recognize it because your focus is always on others. You can't hear from God if your focus is not on Him for you. God will eventually get your attention one way or the other. Focusing on everybody will lead you in the wrong direction with leaning on your own understanding verse God understanding. Focus on God to see what He has already ordained for your life.

Galatians 6:3-5

If you think you are too important to help someone, you are only fooling yourself. You are not that important. Pay careful attention to your own work, for then you will get the satisfaction of a job well done, and you won't need to compare yourself to anyone else. For we are each responsible for our own conduct.

Forgive before Rest

Allow your heart not to be troubled when going to bed. Forgiveness should be acceptable in our life at some point because God forgive when we have not learned from the first time. We can't allow our heart to govern our thoughts our minds are the battlefield. Sometimes we say we forgive someone and still hold on to the problem. Forgiveness is not for the other person but to set you free from bondage.

Mark 11:25

But when you are praying, first forgive anyone you are holding a grudge against, so that your Father in heaven will forgive your sins, too.

Matthew 6:15

But if you refuse to forgive others, your Father will not forgive your sins.

Clean the Clutter

Sometimes we may need to clean the clutter in our path in order to give God our attention and have a better understanding of what God wants us to do. We block our own blessing sometimes and blame everybody for our wrong decision making. Clear the way.

1 Corinthians 14:40

But be sure that everything is done properly and in order.

"Mind Wonder"

We go through things at times and we wonder why? People hurt us at times and we wonder why? When things don't go our way, we wonder why? Its two reasons why we go through what we go through, one we put ourselves in situations not rooted in God's Word and second we have growing pains the pains we face in life will only make us a stronger man or woman.

1 Peter 5:10

In his kindness God called you to share in his eternal glory by means of Christ Jesus. So after you have suffered a little while, he will restore, support, and strengthen you, and he will place you on a firm foundation.

Day 11

"Life Troubles"

When life troubles loom over us, we tend to lose our focus and sense of perspective, not remembering God has already fought our battles in life. We just need to trust in him and know He sent His only son Jesus Christ to die for us.

John 16:33

I have told you all this so that you may have peace in me. Here on earth you will have many trials and sorrows. But take heart, because I have overcome the world.

"Dark vs. Light"

What we do in the dark will come to light. No matter how much we think we can hide in the dark, eventually our light will shine not only to ourselves but to the world of shame.

John 8:12

Jesus spoke to the people once more and said, I am the light of the world. If you follow me, you won't have to walk in darkness, because you will have the light that leads to life.

Day 13

"It's for You"

What God has for you, it's for you. When God open a door for us, no man can close it. No matter what battle flare in our life, trust Him as small as a mustard seed. He is the Greater God in us. He will bless us what is promise to us in His plan. It's worth waiting on God, He has everything we need.

Jeremiah 29:11

For I know the plans I have for you, says the Lord. They are plans for good and not for disaster, to give you a future and a hope.

"Is it Worth It"

Is it worth hurting someone that you know is true to you? Is it worth cheating, when you can end the relationship? Think, what if someone hurt you, how would you feel? Treat people as you want to be treated. No matter how tough or big someone may act everyone has feelings at some point. Through every pain and hurt God is a healer that heals our wounds.

Luke 6:31

Do to others as you would like them to do to you.

Day 15

"First or Last"

Is God first or last in your life? People plan their day without God daily. People wake up and rush getting ready for whatever he or she have plan without God involved. People spend money and never bless someone else for the day. One thing people will do is the minute something happen God is the first name they call. We must stop putting God on the back burner and put him first.

Matthew 6:33

Seek the Kingdom of God above all else, and live righteously, and he will give you everything you need.

Day 16

"Positive Change"

It's NEVER too late today to change for the positive. EVEN your negative can be a positive depends on your mindset and how you look at your current circumstance. No matter what friends, family, colleagues, and anybody else think of you, know God loves you no matter what you been through. Change because you know it's the right path of success for you.

Galatians 2:20

My old self has been crucified with Christ. It is no longer I who live, but Christ lives in me. So I live in this earthly body by trusting in the Son of God, who loved me and gave himself for me.

Day 17

"God has It"

God has the best for us, but we don't want to face any trials and tribulations to get what was promised to us. We have to trust, depend, have faith, and believe in Him. He is our helper, way maker, and provider. God has everything we need and want. He has it all in his hands.

Isaiah 43:2

**When you go through deep waters,
I will be with you.
When you go through rivers of difficulty,
you will not drown.
When you walk through the fire of oppression,
you will not be burned up;
the flames will not consume you.**

"It's not Over"

It's not over until God say it's over. If this is your season to go through that is what will happen. The question is you going to give up, or run the race knowing the end is coming with blessings. It's not over because God has the final answer.

Isaiah 41:13

For I hold you by your right hand—
I, the Lord your God.
And I say to you,
'Don't be afraid. I am here to help you.

Day 19

"Hurt & Pain"

Hurt is pain. Pain does hurt. No matter how many scares you have God is a deliverer of all hurt and pain. God still work miracles regardless of the circumstances and situations. His grace and mercy is new every day.

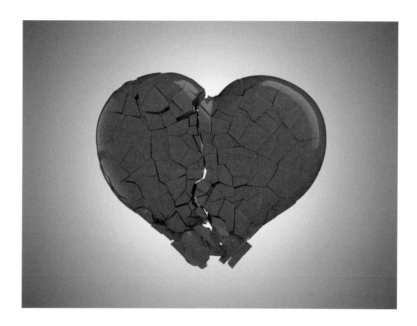

Romans 8:18

Yet what we suffer now is nothing compared to the glory he will reveal to us later.

"There's A Way Hold On"

God heal our mind, body, and soul in His time of recovery through our prayer. Don't allow every tear to be hurt tears but joy. He has a way for everything and there is always a reason why things happen in our life, even when we feel we are doing the right thing. What we think is right in our eyes, does not mean it line up according to His will for us. Just hold on and no every trial and tribulation comes to make us stronger and learn through experiences.

James 1:2-4

Dear brothers and sisters, when troubles of any kind come your way, consider it an opportunity for great joy. For you know that when your faith is tested, your endurance has a chance to grow. So let it grow, for when your endurance is fully developed, you will be perfect and complete, needing nothing.

"Power in the Tongue"

Have you ever regretted something you said as soon as the words flattered out your mouth? We must remember to think a situation out first and pray because we can't take back the words we spoke to someone or people. Words do damage to any relationship. Think before speaking out loud. We have power in the tongue for life or death.

Proverbs 18:21

The tongue can bring death or life; those who love to talk will reap the consequences.

"Clean Record"

Do you think God will heal all your problems before coming into a relationship or commitment with someone? Do you think the person you meet will not have any issues or problems? That is wishful thinking but impossible because no one is perfect. We can avoid situations and circumstances for perfection. If your record is clean, what would you pray for? The person issues or problems can be delivered through you'll praying and trusting in God.

Psalm 51:7

**Purify me from my sins, and I will be clean;
wash me, and I will be whiter than snow.**

Day 23

"Favored"

Favored is not what I have but who has me. Every situation doesn't deserve your tear, so choose what situation deserves your tears. God said weeping endure for a night and joy cometh in the morning. No matter what my facts say because I got a bible that provides me with the truth. Greater He is in me than of the world. Weeping-Possibility and Joy-Absolute. You are favored.

Psalm 90:17

**And may the Lord our God show us his approval
and make our efforts successful.
Yes, make our efforts successful!**

Day 24

"Strength through It All"

After going through so much we become a sponge. It's up to you to soak it up or let it overflow. At the time going through with hurt and pain get in sponge mode. Sponge mode mean anything someone throw at you soak it all up and learn from it gain strength. Don't cry over spilt milk but wipe it up and keep it moving.

Deuteronomy 31:6

So be strong and courageous! Do not be afraid and do not panic before them. For the Lord your God will personally go ahead of you. He will neither fail you nor abandon you.

"Respect"

Why want respect from others when you don't respect yourself? In order to get respect two things need to fall in line. First know what respect is and second understand the concept of respect before respecting yourself and you wanting people to respect you.

Matthew 7:12

Do to others whatever you would like them to do to you. This is the essence of all that is taught in the law and the prophets.

"Expectations"

We have expectations of people and hurt no one but ourselves. We expect someone to be someone they are not or will never be. Yes, we should expect something's out a person but not expect everything because what we will do. God has expectations of us but do we do it all the time? When you expect someone to do something inform them what expectations you have of them and see how it will work out for the both of you. Pray and turn it over to Jesus. He will do what is best.

Proverbs 24:14

**In the same way, wisdom is sweet to your soul.
If you find it, you will have a bright future,
and your hopes will not be cut short.**

Day 27

"Trust in Man"

We hurt everyday from worldly things in the world of man. We put our trust in Man and Man fail us in no time when we least expect it. Then we want to say "Why this happen when we know it was wrong from the start. God gave us knowledge and wisdom. See Man will dish out gifts to get our attention and shame us when we least expect it. God rewards and no Man can take it away.

Jeremiah 17:5

This is what the Lord says:
Cursed are those who put their trust in mere humans,
who rely on human strength
and turn their hearts away from the Lord.

Day 28

"Life"

Never ask for nothing you demand of yourself from others. For instance you want honesty, love, respect, loyalty, peace, ambitious, and wealth but not willing to provide it from your end. If you can't hold yourself accountable and responsible of these areas, why expect to receive it? Everything starts within you all with God guidance.

Ephesians 2:8-9

God saved you by his grace when you believed. And you can't take credit for this; it is a gift from God. Salvation is not a reward for the good things we have done, so none of us can boast about it.

Day 29

"Today Matters"

No matter what you faced yesterday or who hurt you in the past, God is still with you through it all. God paid the price for your healing and pain don't last forever. Think about today and where you are heading now for the future after being hurt. Don't give up keep striving and know God is able in all ways.

Matthew 6:34

So don't worry about tomorrow, for tomorrow will bring its own worries. Today's trouble is enough for today.

"Useless Things"

Favored is not what I own but it's who has me of why I am favored. Having a relationship with Jesus will only last forever. The things I own is materialistic and can be taken at any given day. God is a God of unconditional love and will bless us with our needs and wants in His time.

Matthew 6:33

Seek the Kingdom of God above all else, and live righteously, and he will give you everything you need.

"Be Careful & Mindful"

Life is what you make of it. It can be good or bad. Don't take advantage of no one or take someone for granted and think it's cool. Don't mistreat people because of their culture. Allow no one to take control of you. Life is like a globe we will reap what we sow double or triple of what you have done to someone. It is worth going through. God don't take control or boss us around. God is so loved. Analyze how you really treat others in the world. What if God was a God that mistreated us for all we do? Be Careful and Mindful.

Luke 6:31

Do to others as you would like them to do to you.

"Strive"

Successful people are people who have fell but never quit regardless of the obstacle or hurdle in their way. If we give up every time an obstacle arises in our way, how can we accomplish our goal? Sometimes an obstacle can be for our good because God covered us from going the way we planned to go. The way we planned could have been danger. God will do what is best for us.

1 Timothy 4:10

This is why we work hard and continue to struggle, for our hope is in the living God, who is the Savior of all people and particularly of all believers.

"Friends"

We all say we have friends. Are our friends there when we really need them? Have your friend and you showed each other how much you'll appreciate each other as the friends or the friendship is a way one street? Friends will only tell you what make them sound good. Also, friends will tell you something to make you feel good about yourself. A real friend will be honest with you, when you know you are wrong. You can run with your friends and end up going to hell. When you run with Jesus it will last forever and you will enter the gates of heaven. Choose and make the best decision for you and your family. Think about what would last forever and prosper.

John 15:13

There is no greater love than to lay down one's life for one's friends.

"Pray vs. Judge"

Why when we come to a mind set to begin our life serving God, we can start gossiping and judging others like we are now better than them because they choose to still live in their lifestyle of doing what they want to do without God? That is not right - who are we to judge. When we were doing this and that and others were trying to teach us, months ago, we were not ready. If we were to pull our own cover back, it will be a trail from here to Jamaica, if not longer. But know one thing, God is a God of His word and will cast it all away. We just need to continue to pray for the deliverance of people attached to us, a change according to God's will and not our ways. When you change your perception, you can change your life. Don't worry about what people may say because you are changing for the better. Watch your blessings and eventually one day your friends, family, and others will try Jesus for themselves because of all the blessings you're receiving.

James 5:16

Confess your sins to each other and pray for each other so that you may be healed. The earnest prayer of a righteous person has great power and produces wonderful results.

Matthew 7:1-2

Do not judge others, and you will not be judged. For you will be treated as you treat others. The standard you use in judging is the standard by which you will be judged.

"Power"

We have the power to move the enemy out of our house. Sometimes, you got to talk to the enemy and let him know you have all power to defeat him anytime he (Satan) tries you, or anything in your house. When Satan knows he can't attack you, he starts planning and working on everything that is attached to you. Tell him "get out of your house" because he is wasting his time trying to destroy this house. Satan only has power if you allow him to be the strong man in your home. Tell him the Holy Spirit lives in here in the name of Jesus, and cast each and every spirit back to the pit of Hell. Tell him to go, go, go, go, go, you have had enough of him taking over you and your home. You have been down, and carrying heavy burdens and you're tired. Go before God and ask for forgiveness. Tell Him you need Him to help you, guide and direct you because you can't do it alone, you've tried and it's not working. God's Grace and Mercy come to let us know we are not alone. We use our tongue to speak all other things, but when it's time to speak power over us and our home, we don't use it for the good gossip. Power is in our tongue through every trial and tribulation.

Acts 1:8

But you will receive power when the Holy Spirit comes upon you. And you will be my witnesses, telling people about me everywhere—in Jerusalem, throughout Judea, in Samaria, and to the ends of the earth.

"Love God"

Don't expect someone to truly love you for you until they love God for who He is. He loves us unconditionally in our mess. We give up on him but he never leave nor forsake us but still love us. He chose us but it's up to us to choose him at some point in our life. But when you stop worrying about what the world think or say about you, you will then see and realize the big picture of what really matter and what will last forever. You can accept Jesus as your Lord and savior (if you have not yet), repent and let it go, forgive and move on (because we are not perfect), pray not only in time of trouble or when you want something, but always even if it's just his name "Jesus or "Lord, I thank you, you can love God and know you covered by the best, allow him to direct your path, guide you daily, strengthen your weakness, study his word so you can bear fruit and testify how good he is to you, experience and observe circumstances & situations to encourage the unbelievers to become believers, gain power to defeat the enemy, God strengthen and give wisdom to us through trials, tribulations and tests when they come but know and understand the difference when Satan come it's to kill and destroy, realize when the enemy uses others to come up against you and your flesh, take responsibility and accountability for your own actions of your decisions (not always the enemy it's just you being and doing you), allow no one actions to influence you to react out the will of God, and everything else pertaining you will fall in line, if its according to his will and plan for you. In order for this to align and strive for the best a person as an individual have to want a change in their life. No change is successful or will last unless through Jesus and the Father (God) changeable hands. So who the world see you as is irrelevant and countless, but who God see you as is what will last forever with peace, love, happiness, and blessing abundantly will rain upon you.

1 John 4:16

We know how much God loves us, and we have put our trust in his love. God is love, and all who live in love live in God, and God lives in them.

"Two-Way Street"

Respect is earned. Honesty is appreciated. Loyalty is in returned. We meet some people for a climate, season, and short-term, long-term and eternal life. We want people to respect us but we don't even respect ourselves. We ask for honesty but reality can't handle it and not honest with ourselves. Loyalty plays a big part in our life but we have to realize if you not loyal, why want someone to be loyal to you. If you are loyal but not receiving loyalty back after awhile something need to be address and pray asking God for guidance.

Philippians 2:3

Don't be selfish; don't try to impress others. Be humble, thinking of others as better than yourselves.

Day 38

"Going Through"

Sometimes we make the wrong decisions and choices in life and must be strong enough to face whatever circumstance it turns out to be. Do you ever think about how blessed you really are at the end of each day in spite of your situation? Do your good outweigh your bad? No matter what the day brings there is one person that is always with you name God. He will dispatch his angels to cover us. However, we can't continue to do the same thing through the years and think we will still be blessed. What we do to others we will reap what we sow in due time. What we don't live and see our children will eventually face situations on our behalf far as the parent. We suppose to be a role model and set examples for our children to live a better life then us. There are some things in our life we just have to let it go and move on. Something's God separate us from and we as humans choose to go backwards. That's where we block our own blessings. We are not perfect but we can avoid a lot of negatively we do and what we allow in our life. If someone presence don't bring value into your life, then when they are gone you won't be missing nothing. We have to think before taking actions.

Matthew 6:31

So don't worry about these things, saying, What will we eat? What will we drink? What will we wear?

"Lying"

Sometimes we have a misconception about someone telling a lie or lying. We not talking about surprises or something we need to tell a lie about because something we are planning for some event or etc... We are talking about serious situations that cause hurt and pain in our life. People like to say "some things you have to lie about so you won't hurt that person. Not true in the long run you hurt them even more by not confessing the truth from the start and prolonged it by hiding it. God show up for his people right on time. If you ask someone a question, and they give you a response, what they told you is what they want you to know if you are not entitled to know what's going on with that person or people. They are not lying to you but provided you with information they felt like telling you. However, there are stipulations to this because some of us are entitled to know the truth depending on our relationship with that person or people. (Example: wife, husband, fiancée, love ones, and anyone you have a relationship with and ya'll agree to be honest and truthful to each other). If you don't ask a question, and someone tells you something and later the truth come out. That is a lie because you didn't even ask they volunteer information to you. If you always telling me a lie, what make me think you won't lie on me? A person that tells a lie when it's the truth and believe they own lie is a composer liar. That is a bad spirit. When you keep lying day after day it will eventually catch up to you. That's a routine in your mind and you take action, but one day you will forget your own routine and the truth will then come to light. God is a good God. The day you get a heart desire to change from your fleshly and evil spirits ways, God changing hands is there for the positive change. It is worth the change because peace, joy, and happiness live within you, in spite of any other trials and tribulations that may arise.

Colossians 3:9-10

Don't lie to each other, for you have stripped off your old sinful nature and all its wicked deeds. Put on your new nature, and be renewed as you learn to know your Creator and become like him.

"Follower"

Anyone that follow a crowd never get ahead of the crowd but the one who walk alone end up in places no one has never been. We should be following Jesus who will lead us on the right path and direction. It's your choice of who you want to follow daily Jesus or the world.

John 8:12

Jesus spoke to the people once more and said, I am the light of the world. If you follow me, you won't have to walk in darkness, because you will have the light that leads to life.

30 Years of doing the Devil's work:

I want to share how I transitioned myself from doing the devil's work to now being fully committed to the one that died for us all (Jesus Christ). For many years, I was lying, cheating, stealing, and having more than one woman; I thought it was all about me. I was assuming that I was doing everything the correct way and was enjoying life. I was doing the devil's work along with the rest of the world.

Although I believed in God, I had chosen not to live for Him in the way that I should have. I was being blessed, but was not experiencing the blessing because I was serving the devil. Then, one day, everything came crashing down on and around me. I had begun to struggle a lot and I did not want to ask for help from any one because I was blaming others for what was, in reality, my actions. I was feeling alone and empty. Now that I know right from wrong and look back at my past, I know the devil was telling Jesus, "Look at this young man called Your son - he is one of my favorites because of all the sins he has committed". I know that Jesus was allowing me to face some things to see if I would make the choice to serve Him each day. I am glad that God has Grace and Mercy over us and does not make us pay back for all of the sins that we have done.

I am 32 years old, and have been free of the devil's work for two years. I tell myself that I will get right with the Lord this day. I will be faithful to one woman and I have been committed to her and only her for 3 years now. I will stop lying about the mistakes that I have made and will "man up" to my actions. I will have feelings for others instead of thinking only about myself.

I try to lead by example and I strive to share my past with others my age and younger, so that they will know that the road they are going down is not worth it. I try to show them that I was going down the same path that they are traveling, but now, I do not travel that path any more. I do not do what the rest of the world does; I walk the path that leads to God because God is the head of my life and not the tail. I encourage others to walk the same path because it takes a strong, discipline individual to change their life around for the better, for God.

Daily, I pray and ask God to keep my family and me safe in His hands. God has been blessing me in many ways and I know there is more to come. I believe that God will continue to bless me as long as I am living right and being committed to Him.

When I committed myself to Jesus Christ, I had to forgive myself and I had to ask God to forgive me for all of the sins I had committed. I also had to listen to the Holy Spirit and ask forgiveness from those that I had hurt in the past. Asking for forgiveness and being forgiven was like a heavy weight being lifted off of my shoulders and I had to rejoice because I felt like I was reborn. There is no feeling like the feeling of being set free - life is great every day now because I know I have Jesus in my corner.

I have a family that is made up of six beautiful, highly intelligent children and a beautiful fiancée, who is an Accountant and has graduated from Law school. I am USMC military veteran who is doing the following all at the same time: 1.) Pursuing a degree in Business with a 3.8 GPA, 2.) Attending truck driver's school part-time, and 3.) Studying to become a Highway Patrol Officer. I am successfully accomplishing all of these things through my faith in God and the support of my family, who believes in me and keeps me straight. I want to encourage everyone to say, "No devil, get away from me - I now live for the Lord. You and your spirits must go away - I cast you back to the pit of hell in the name of Jesus." Trust in the Lord to keep the evil spirits away by His word, which is in the Bible. I would like to say thank you to my sister for considering me as a living testimony for her first book to the world.

God Bless.

Thank You

I would first like to thank God for allowing this book to be successful and on time for His people across the world including myself. I give special thanks to my significant other for motivating and listening to me through this journey, Apostle Monica Boykin for being that spiritual and encouraging leader of God, Prophet Fran McFadden for prophesying God word to me as the spirit flow, my spiritual brother/friend who has encouraged, motivated, and helped me go forward with organizing this special book. I also give thanks to a special woman who has helped me; I call her my technical proof reader. I thank my mother for being that strong role model through the years. Thanks to all my fans that supported and encouraged me along this journey of writing my first book. I have met numerous of people of all cultures from working and traveling across the world and I pray everyone finds understanding, wisdom, and motivation after reading the scriptures and encouragement on each page. Before reading, we should focus on God and enter the book with expectancy, so we can hear from God. We should also document our thoughts and words – so that we can encourage and motivate someone along their journey. God is good all of the time and all of the time, God is good. Peace, Love, and Happiness to everyone.

Trust God through It All! Victory Is Yours!

Printed in the United States
By Bookmasters